Self-Esteem

Comprehensive Handbook On Developing Confidence And Strategies For Immediate Enhancement Of Self-Worth

(Effective Strategies For Enhancing Self-Esteem And Confidence In Both Genders)

Carroll Roberson

TABLE OF CONTENT

What Is Your Self-Perception?...................................1

Maximizing Introversion..29

Promoting A Optimistic Mental Attitude. 43

Objective Establishment And The Endeavor Towards Accomplishing Those Objectives. 62

Self-Esteem Strategy 1 – Acquiring Insight Into The Origins Of Your Emotional State..................70

What Does Not Ascertain Or Define One's Intrinsic Value Or Personal Worth 77

The Distinction Between Self-Esteem And Confidence...86

Positive Thinking.. 101

What Is Your Self-Perception?

The assertion that "the world is predominantly male-dominated" is a frequently echoed sentiment that profoundly affects many men, particularly those who struggle with their sense of self-assurance and self-worth. Despite the acknowledgment of gender equality, the male population continues to face significant demands across various domains of life. Males are consistently held to the societal standard of delivering optimal performance in various domains including corporate, athletic, entertainment, and similar spheres. This implicit anticipation challenges men to engage in a competitive mindset, while the principle of "survival of the fittest" continues to persist as the prevailing standard.

This presents a significant hurdle for men who experience feelings of insecurity and possess limited self-confidence and self-worth, thereby hindering their ability to fully exploit their capabilities. Many individuals, despite the pressures and obligations imposed by society, possess the capacity to venture into the world and openly express their intentions to achieve great success. This is not due to their inability or lack of competence, but rather stems from their diminished self-esteem and absence of self-assurance.

Indeed, does a discrepancy truly exist between the pair? Is it possible to enhance either one, or perhaps both of them?

The objective of this eBook is to offer you a comprehensive comprehension of the principles of self-esteem and self-confidence, with the intention of assisting you in surmounting any obstacles that may impede your progress towards your goals and utmost potential. By doing so, it will enable you to assert your deserving place in society.

It is our aspiration that following the perusal of this literature, you will amass an ample amount of knowledge enabling you to overcome not only shyness and inhibitions, but also various impediments that hinder your ability to realize your utmost potential.

Chapter Four: A Comparison of Self-Esteem and Self-Confidence

Many individuals often conflate the concepts of self-esteem and self-confidence. Indeed, the topic of confidence often intertwines with that of self-esteem, as many individuals interchangeably use these terms in their conversations. Many individuals easily fall into the misconception that self-esteem and confidence are interchangeable. No, they\'re not. They are completely distinct entities. They do affect oneself; that is a shared characteristic they possess. However, in terms of their operational procedures, impact, and application, they fundamentally diverge from one another.

It is imperative to comprehend the distinction between self-esteem and self-confidence, as well as their interconnectedness. By comprehending and understanding the dynamics of these two concepts within the context of your own existence, you can construct an effective framework that would empower you to lead a life imbued with heightened self-assurance. That is the definitive objective we aim to achieve. However, before we can attain that objective, it is imperative that we first acknowledge and tackle the issue of self-esteem.

What is Self-Esteem?

Self-esteem is the assessment you make of your own worth. You reflect upon your own self, and you formulate various assessments. You construct a tale or personal account delineating your intrinsic worth as an individual, your position in society, and your significance. Do you possess the qualities and attributes that would warrant making sacrifices on your behalf? Do you merit a considerable amount of anything? How important are you?

These inquiries pertain to one's self-worth. These questions pertain to one's personal values, wherein an individual assigns worth to oneself.

What is self-confidence? Self-assurance is the outward manifestation of the sense of value, position, significance, and efficacy one experiences. Although self-esteem resides solely within an individual, manifesting in a subtle exchange of ideas and personal introspection that remains hidden from the general public, self-confidence is prominently displayed in the external sphere.

Allow me to rephrase: If you were to hold the belief that you are entirely unsuccessful, your subsequent behavior would likely be that of an individual predisposed to failure. You begin to engage in work with an apparent lack of self-worth and a lack of self-respect.

Self-assurance relies on the outward indications one conveys to the external environment, influencing the perception and appraisal of oneself. As evident from the context, self-confidence and self-esteem are inherently interconnected; they both emanate from a common source. While the former is solely confined within oneself, the latter pertains to external matters and is of public nature. This is what ultimately causes perplexity. There is a prevalent belief among many individuals that these entities are indistinguishable. While they do originate from a common source, it is important to note that self-esteem is an inherently internal attribute.

Now, let us frame it in this manner, individuals may perceive you as being accomplished. There is a possibility that individuals may perceive you as affluent, influential, and extraordinary. All of these assessments are of an external nature. Nevertheless, if one holds the belief that they possess no value and are merely a heap of refuse, it is unlikely that any form of external validation will successfully alleviate their self-esteem issues. Self-esteem, in essence, pertains to the inherent assessment of one's value, encompassing an individual narrative regarding their significance, position in society, and overall worth.

Self-esteem refers to the internal sense of one's own confidence.

I do not intend to create any confusion, however, if you are seeking a concise explanation of self-esteem, it can be defined as the internalization of self-assurance. You recognize your inherent worth as an individual and hold the belief that you possess intrinsic value. You can do it. You possess the necessary qualities; you are indeed a rightful member, and so forth and so on. It constitutes the internal manifestation of your inherent capabilities and the intrinsic worth that you assign to yourself.

Nevertheless, it is crucial to acknowledge that self-esteem ultimately stems from one's individual assessment or evaluation. It pertains to personal matters; it is internalized. You prioritize your intrinsic worth and concentrate on defining your value.

The Extrinsic Factors Influencing Self-Assurance

If the sense of self-worth is internalized as self-confidence, then self-confidence is manifested as an external display of self-esteem. Now, I must avoid any potential confusion, but given that your self-esteem is the foundational element shaping your personality, it logically follows that your actions in relation to the external world are a manifestation or a reflection of your internal state. Put simply, it commences with your self-worth and the beliefs you opt to embrace concerning your own personhood. It commences with the articulation of your personal narrative pertaining to your position within the global context, your intrinsic worth, significance, and the scope of your abilities. Nevertheless, it subsequently advances and resolves on its own.

What is the tangible evidence or explicit expression of this? What is the perception of the global populace? The external world would discern particular indications. It would be advantageous to take heed of your body language. Do you exude an aura of self-assurance that gives others the impression of your unwavering confidence in your capacity to accomplish tasks? Alternatively, would you consider being contented with the knowledge that you are effectively informed on the subject matter? Does your nonverbal communication align with or indicate this?

Individuals would also be inclined to attend to your facial gestures. Do you experience difficulty maintaining direct eye contact with others? Do you consistently experience the need to avert your gaze due to feelings of embarrassment? Do you struggle to convey specific expressions? In addition, these findings can be interpreted as confident individuals often exhibit specific facial expressions. Their intention is not to assert dominance over others; rather, they do not seek to impose their confidence upon others through forceful means. On the contrary, their faith is inherent. It instills a sense of calmness in individuals, whilst simultaneously projecting a steadfast internal demeanor.

Moreover, self-assurance is demonstrated in our manner of addressing circumstances. In circumstances where an embarrassing incident unfolds, or a situation arises that may potentially give rise to conflict, is it your natural inclination to promptly withdraw or offer an apology? Does your instinct promptly assign blame, attempting to conceal any errors and relying on others not to notice your mistake? The manner in which you navigate circumstances ultimately influences the level of credibility you command from others.

If you possess a proactive nature, individuals would take notice and lend their full attention, as individuals with such qualities are rare. Most people are passive. The manner in which you navigate circumstances is directly influenced by the extent of your self-assurance.

The selection of your words serves as an indication of your level of self-assurance. It is a common observation that individuals may refrain from expressing their lack of financial resources by stating, "I do not possess any monetary means." It is deemed infeasible." Alternatively, alternate expressions are employed. They inquire, "How may I accomplish such a task?" "What strategies can I employ to generate the necessary funds?" In essence, they inquire about potential solutions that may pave the way for their desired outcome to materialize.

Contrast this with the use of derogatory remarks, namely stating, "I am unable to afford it." I\'m broke. Regrettably, it is highly unlikely to occur." With whom of these individuals would you prefer to socialize? I thought so.

Ultimately, an additional external element of self-assurance pertains to one's verbal expression. If you are an individual who lacks the ability to communicate with sufficient assertiveness that would inspire trust in your abilities, this can present a concern. Individuals will not seek your guidance or advice. Individuals will not seek you out for the purpose of finding inspiration. How can you fulfill their expectations when it is apparent that you lack knowledge and understanding on the subject matter? Or at the very least, do you fail to exhibit indications that convey your confidence in the correctness of your statements and convictions?

To what extent do these external indicators of self-assurance hold significance? They hold significance due to their ability to exert influence on others and generate outcomes. Do bear in mind that acting with self-assurance is not merely a result of idleness or lack of preferable alternatives. Self-assurance is not merely a superficial designation or ornamentation, but instead holds substantive significance. It does not resemble a vibrant jacket that one adorns, eliciting expressions of praise from onlookers. Rather, it exerts a discernible influence on those in proximity. Once this effect is induced, it subsequently accumulates to alter your role.

Could you please explain how this situation unfolds? Indeed, when you project outward expressions of confidence, you influence individuals in such a manner that engenders trust. They experience an increase in their level of comfort; they develop a greater sense of familiarity. They exhibit a greater inclination towards assistance; these cumulative factors contribute to increasingly elevated levels of reverence. Furthermore, these collective factors instill the perception that you are an integral member of their team, and conversely, they feel like esteemed members of your team, thus establishing a strong sense of connection between all parties involved.

To put it differently, a sense of assurance empowers individuals to not only transform their environment, but also enhance their immediate circumstances. The significance of self-confidence cannot be overstated, as it is crucial to recognize that the world tends to be indifferent towards individual emotions. Truly, one may experience a sense of great strength, yet it remains inconsequential if it fails to translate into tangible behaviors. You are expending futile efforts as the world solely allocates recognition to one's actions.

One approach to accomplishing tasks is by exerting enough influence or inspiring others to act on your instructions or alter their behavior. Do you understand the functioning of this process? That is the manner in which society evaluates individuals. That is how society evaluates individuals. The matter at hand is entirely objective; it pertains strictly to the achievement of outcomes. All this talk about feelings, emotions, what could've happened, what should have happened or what they have intended, all that is rubbish.

None of that matters. The only thing of significance in terms of the world is the actions you have taken. What steps did you take to alter your environment? To what extent did your presence influence those in your vicinity? Has there been a cessation in the alteration of people's behavior? Put simply, the international community observes the intricacies of human interactions and the subsequent cascade of events that materialize through various actions. Put differently, this is unequivocal. This is not conjectural; this is not supposition. Whether or not you have undertaken an action remains undetermined. Either you had exerted an influence, or you simply did not.

The significance of self-confidence becomes evident as it profoundly alters one's perception of reality from an objective standpoint. When one exerts influence upon others, their behavior can be altered, facilitating progress towards a shared objective. You may commence interpersonal communication with the aim of effectuating targeted alterations. It is important to bear in mind that these changes may yield either favorable or unfavorable outcomes. That's not the point. The essence lies in the fact that the world evaluates individuals solely based on their outcome achievements. This can be positive results, as well as negative results.

Chapter 5

It is solely within the confines of our cognition.

Direct one's attention towards the positive aspects

We all encounter challenging circumstances in life, as it is an inevitable aspect of our existence.

Typically, the circumstances do not lend themselves to a state of luxury. Ultimately, life is what you choose to make of it and through reframing your perspective, you can shape it accordingly.

Maintaining a positive attitude during challenging times can make a significant difference, just as focusing on the positive aspects can have a profound impact.

and helps you navigate challenging circumstances with a smile.

Notwithstanding, the primary concern is "how can one maintain a positive outlook in the face of challenging circumstances?"

"Is it challenging to come?" Maintaining a positive attitude during moments like this is crucial.

Your thoughts, although they should be prioritized, you must now deliberate with unwavering positivity.

fore. One can cultivate a positive outlook by shifting their focus away from personal troubles and concerns, and instead redirecting their attention towards other matters.

Exercising cognitive faculties, this becomes especially apparent during moments of emotional duress, when one is experiencing a difficult day.

I am experiencing a sense of frustration towards myself and feel compelled to sit down and weep. Presented herewith are a selection of invaluable recommendations for

Maintaining an unwavering perspective of inspiration in life irrespective of the prevailing circumstances.

• If you find yourself in the company of negative individuals, it is best to disengage from their presence.

For them, cynicism possesses a means of spreading from one individual to another and shall invariably exert influence.

Are you aligned with them?

• It is advised not to engage in prolonged television viewing sessions, as the news can be distressing.

Encouraging, law enforcement establishments showcase brutality and conflictuality in various forms, which can be observed in nearly every television program. Should you choose to watch television

As an illustration of a more optimistic program, a nature documentary showcasing the breathtaking

The complete splendor of the world or a satirical imitation.

• Devote ample amounts of time to your loved ones, both family members and friends, in order to achieve a sense of fulfillment.

Collaborate on an activity that is mutually cherished by all members and make arrangements for a familial gathering in the near future.

Frequency of occurrence per week, providing opportunities for social interaction.

• During moments of emotional distress and the onset of skepticism, direct your attention towards

Listen to a motivational audio disc or recite affirmations to yourself to restore a positive and uplifting mindset.

frame of mind.

- Allocate time each day to engage in activities that bring you joy and fulfillment.

Does not anticipate you to make decisions or choices, leading to a sense of relaxation.

without limit.

- Endeavor to achieve something outside of your usual routine, an endeavor that is completely unexpected

Deviate from the ordinary and unconventional; explore alternative recreational pursuits or engage in a different game or pastime.

I have never harbored a desire to engage in.

- Engage in physical activity, such as taking a leisurely walk outdoors.

Furthermore, individuals have the complete freedom to either visit the recreational center or engage in activities such as yoga.

ga.

• Establish clear objectives for yourself in order to achieve exceptional results, and once you attain a goal, acknowledge your accomplishment by giving yourself a

There is minimal compensation provided for undertaking such action.

• Acquire techniques that empower you to redirect your attention and focus

swiftly complete an errand in close proximity.

• Employ affirmations throughout the day to instill confidence and positivity.

contemplations and emotions.

• In the face of adverse circumstances, it is important to consistently strive to find the most favorable aspects, even if the situation may not align with our expectations.

Upon diligent search, it is anticipated that you may ascertain that they are not as one initially perceived.

Despite their apparent awfulness.

• Please be advised that the current circumstance is only temporary, and it shall improve in due course.

There are no bounds to your potential in the sky.

With unwavering dedication, one can attain whatever they set their sights on, as the vast expanse above serves as the ultimate limit, and abstaining from surrendering is key to progress.

If one diligently follows a series of fundamental steps, remarkable achievements can be accomplished in various endeavors throughout one's lifetime. The

The modality of advancing lies primarily in full commitment towards achieving one's desired objectives, thereby ensuring the attainment of one's goals.

Direct your efforts towards undertaking the necessary strides to accomplish your desired objectives and effectuate personal transformation.

Utilize a systematic approach and adhere to this novel methodology until the desired outcome is achieved. The means

The process of pursuing them is relatively straightforward and adjustments can be made easily in order to determine your accommodation.

In order to attain success in any endeavor one encounters in life, let us now proceed to examine the aforementioned steps.

Maximizing Introversion

There is a considerable population of introverts who consistently experience a sense of displacement in various settings, particularly in the workplace, public venues, and occasionally within social gatherings. The issue lies in the fact that conversations are often dominated by individuals seeking to assert themselves or generate amusement. Regrettably, establishing meaningful connections with most individuals through humor is not their area of expertise. Frequently, prior to participating in a group discussion or work meeting, they are commonly preconceived as being the "solitary," reserved, timid, and occasionally unsociable individual. This societal stigma further exacerbates the challenges faced by individuals who seek solitude, hindering their ability to integrate seamlessly into social circles, let alone make strides in their professional careers. They are increasingly realizing that accomplishment is exclusively attainable by individuals who possess the ability to confidently captivate an audience and decisively execute novel concepts. Please prepare yourself, as there will be alterations in the near future.

As individuals who possess introverted traits are increasingly cognizant of the perceived preference for extraverted personalities, they are also coming to understand that their introversion does not present any form of drawback or disadvantage. It is indeed a highly effective tool and underutilized asset that can be exclusively accessed by the reticent individuals—an advantage for introverts. The workforce is the primary domain in which each individual who actively contributes to society dedicates a significant portion of their day. The taciturn individuals possess inherent skills that can be employed to their advantage, thereby allowing them to make the most out of the situation.

Overcome Shyness

The reserved individuals do not inherently possess an aversion to engaging in conversation with individuals outside their immediate circle, although it is not uncommon to encounter some degree of timidity among them. To some you are indeed shy, overcoming it is a task they must face first. Unlike the general populace, introverts do not particularly value being thrust into social situations and relying on their own ability to adapt in order to learn. Additionally, they do not exhibit a positive response when subjected to coercion or intimidation tactics. For those of a reticent disposition, such behavior can be perceived as an act of aggression, serving as further evidence for why individuals feel depleted of their strength and vitality. The most effective approach to addressing shyness entails facilitating a comprehensive comprehension of the situation among individuals with introverted tendencies. The inquiries as to reasons for and against should be addressed.

Why should you speak? Because you have ideas. Indeed, there exist alternative strategies that can effectively advance the objectives of the company while mitigating excessive risk. Your intention is not to seek praise or idolization, but rather to actively contribute to the workforce and receive appropriate recognition for your contributions. Have you ever encountered a scenario where you abstained from expressing your ideas, resulting in the governing body selecting an idea considerably inferior to your own? Do the words "My idea was better" sound familiar? This ill-advised endeavor not only materialized, but its flawed inception and inherent risk had detrimental repercussions on the collective efforts of others, including your own. The environment is characterized by excessive commotion, which possesses the potential to excessively stimulate individuals with introverted tendencies. Should you choose not to advocate for yourself for the purpose of gaining acknowledgement, it is recommended that you instead voice your thoughts in order to diminish the turmoil that interferes with your ability to focus and find solace.

Engaging in conversation can evoke fear in certain individuals due to the spontaneous nature of casual discourse, wherein topics can swiftly transition from one to another. Chats are small talks. Furthermore, casual conversations exhibit the ability to shift topics abruptly and seamlessly. All individuals are anticipated to familiarize themselves and actively participate in various topics. Introverts encounter difficulty in navigating through this process. In addition to requiring ample time for contemplation before speaking, their knowledge of office "news" or gossip is severely restricted. However, interpersonal interaction serves as the key factor in reducing social anxiety.

Talk about work. Engage in a private dialogue with a coworker within the confines of our workplace. The setting holds significant importance, as it effectively conveys to the participants that the conversation revolves around the topic of their respective work and the measures he can undertake to offer assistance. Discussing the job will be beneficial for you, as an introvert, since it will provide you with a comprehensive understanding of the job and enable you to respond effortlessly to any related inquiries. It further diminishes the likelihood of engaging in casual conversations. In this scenario, you will have the opportunity to regulate the course of the conversation, which contrasts with the experience of being in a group meeting where the direction of the conversation may emanate from various sources, potentially leading to feelings of being overwhelmed. It is essential that you retain this sense of control.

At this point, you might be inclined to contemplate the manner in which one should approach public speaking. Never fear. You merely need to recollect the acquired capability of maintaining composure that you assimilated during your individualized discourse. It may come as a revelation to you that introverts find one-on-one conversations particularly challenging. In contrast to that, delivering a speech before an audience is akin to an effortless stroll through nature. Why, you ask. It denotes the regulation of the movement. You hold the reins of the conversation's tempo when you speak. One can proceed at a leisurely pace without fear of interruption or being subjected to trivial conversations. Given your expertise on the matter at hand, inquiries can be raised and you would possess the necessary knowledge readily accessible in your mental repository. It falls under your purview while they serve as mere observers. The advantage lies with introverts.

Continue implementing effective strategies.

The success of introverts relies upon their utilization of their inherent abilities to thrive. It is a widely recognized fact that introverted individuals acquire knowledge primarily through observation, possess the ability to perceive without external distractions, and demonstrate productivity in the context of solitude. They excel in an environment where they are devoid of the persistent disturbance commonly found in the workplace. While others may settle for a superficial understanding of a concept, taciturn individuals dive deeper and display unwavering dedication in fully comprehending it. This attribute holds significant value in the eyes of employers, hence it is imperative to make the most of it.

Steve Wozniak is perhaps the most ardent advocate of embracing solitude and working independently. In the confines of his modest workspace at Hewlett Packard, he conceived and developed the Apple computer, an avant-garde technological breakthrough in the realm of computing. Thus far, he has been underscoring the infrequency with which innovation is attained in a collaborative setting. He has a point. Solitude is not purely a condition exclusive to introverted individuals. It serves as a means of shielding oneself from the cacophonous nature of the surrounding milieu. It provides them with an optimal environment that complements their cognitive processes. Devoid of any disturbances, their cognitive faculties are uninterrupted, allowing for heightened productivity.

Work alone. Keep doing that. As an individual with introverted tendencies, you may find yourself confronted by an array of thoughts and ideas that necessitate conveying them in a manner comprehensible to the general populace. Disruptions and interruptions impede the seamless flow of thought and should therefore be minimized. Being alone is a pleasurable pursuit for an introverted individual, thus in the broader context, while engaged in work, one also derives enjoyment. The fortuitous occurrences in life are the ones that can contribute to the success of an introverted individual. This should not be construed as advocating for the elimination of teamwork. Research findings indicate that significantly greater achievements have been attained through individual contributions as opposed to collaborative endeavors. It constitutes a formal request for employees to have the opportunity to retreat to their individual work areas as necessary. The state of being alone can serve as a catalyst for exceptional performance.

It is unnecessary to instruct you to concentrate solely on a single task at any given point, as it is likely that you have already been adhering to this practice. Keep doing it. It ought not to be presumed as being sluggish but rather as being meticulous. One should partition the tasks into more easily handled segments, tackle and comprehend each component, and devise appropriate resolutions. Evaluate the various options by assessing the associated risks and returns to ascertain the optimal solution. This approach provides an optimal means of grasping the assigned tasks, thereby enabling you to confidently hold your position during any meeting and avoid being caught off guard by inquiries. A respectable employer would prioritize the quality of their employees' work over the quantity without hesitation.

Acquire knowledge while maintaining productivity. This should be achievable as reading extensively is often regarded as one of the most cherished leisure activities for introverted individuals. Keep doing it. Continuous learning will forever remain ingrained within the realm of introverts. It not only brings about excitement for a multitude of individuals, but it also serves as a vital instrument for achieving success. Regardless of its simplicity, the potential benefits of any single piece of information may forever remain unknown to you. When the opportune moment arrives, you can be certain that you are prepared and adequately equipped. The realm of introverts may serve as an optimal environment for fostering resilience and readiness in the face of various challenges.

Promoting A Optimistic Mental Attitude.

Defining the term "mindset" can be challenging, considering its intricate nature as a multifaceted framework encompassing cognitive processes and behavioral patterns. Mindsets have the potential to be characterized by confidence or lethargy. This content primarily focuses on the acquisition of skills for altering one's mindset through initial observation.

Your cognitive composition is in a constant state of flux, continuously adjusting to each moment, while simultaneously displaying highly automated characteristics. We all find ourselves subject to the condition of duality, as it pertains to our current state. It is imperative that we acquire the skill of effectively maintaining equilibrium between different components. For instance, suppose you possess the determination to excel and obtain employment at a neighboring law practice in the capacity of a recently graduated attorney. Your level of confidence is most evident when you possess the knowledge that you perform tasks with excellence and are well-regarded by others. Nevertheless, it appears that your consumption of alcohol is becoming increasingly problematic. You commute to your workplace, experience a sense of accomplishment, and conclude the day with the satisfaction of having performed excellently. This constitutes the appropriate mindset. You are presently seated, contemplating the favorable outcome of your accomplishments today. Subsequently, you depart, resulting in a complete shift in your mindset. You succumb to laziness and return to your residence to uncork the bottle of wine. You have now adopted a mental state that is significantly detrimental to your well-being. It is essential that you acquire the skill of maintaining equilibrium. There exist mentalities that elude detection and pose formidable challenges to combat.

Begin contemplating the manner in which you can enact a comprehensive and transformative overhaul. Indeed, one must understand that when endeavoring to effectuate a transformation in one's life, particularly of a significant nature, a considerable amount of deliberate focus and determination are essential elements. There is an inherent connection; a small modification in one's life has the potential to instigate a comprehensive transformation. It is imperative to set ambitious goals that surpass your perceived requirements, as doing so will enable transformative growth. This excessive correction is indispensable in order to attain a minimal degree of alteration. It is imperative that you adopt the notion of necessity to set your sights significantly higher than your initial estimation.

This is due to the inherent difficulty of effecting a mindset shift to wholly reprogram one's thinking, necessitating a broad outlook. Changing one's mindset necessitates a comprehensive evaluation and an unflinchingly honest assessment of one's objectives.

As an illustration, in the pursuit of acquiring greater emotional maturity, endeavor to cultivate a disposition of actively seeking personal growth and progress specifically in this domain. One can cultivate a mindset inclined towards adaptability and resilience, which, if accomplished, would substantially enhance the likelihood of achieving the set objectives. If one desires to cultivate a greater sense of emotional maturity, it is advisable to dedicate time towards discerning and acknowledging, with compassion and benevolence, instances where one may have demonstrated emotional immaturity in the past.

This may require a significant, transformative experience in order to make any lasting impact. A cathartic experience encompasses a range of encounters, spanning from aesthetic experiences to encounters with the natural world. It could also serve as a tremendous opportunity at a sporting event or even an avenue for emotional release in a sexual context. A moment of catharsis can act as a catalyst for change in order to reprogram your mindset; you will need to be motivated to make the change. Human beings exist in a state of disorder and degradation. We do not like change; we like to drift slowly and deny that everything is impermanent.

Each and every mental state experiences impermanence until the point of our demise. It cannot be denied or overlooked. In the event that you experience contentment momentarily, please bear in mind that you may encounter profound unhappiness in the subsequent moment. This serves as a valuable lesson to refrain from excessively attaching ourselves to any specific emotional state. We should primarily be surrendering to the ebb and flow of our emotional encounters. One component of the necessary shift in mindset is the cultivation of assurance. As previously mentioned, confidence plays a pivotal role in determining the success or failure of the process of recalibrating one's mindset. It will ascertain whether you attain success in your endeavors or necessitate a recalibration of your objectives.

Another prevalent shift in mindset pertains to individuals endeavoring to emerge from the depths of depression. This condition represents a chronic illness that results in feelings of sadness and lack of motivation. It causes a significant number of individuals to reside beyond the optimal limits of interpersonal engagement and social involvement. When people are depressed, they become disconnected from the world, and they do not take action. Depression can be defined as a state characterized by a notable absence of motivation and a limited inclination towards taking action. The transformation of an individual with depression can occur through their active engagement and inward drive.

Individuals who are afflicted with depression should consider adopting the following strategies to shift their cognitive perspective. Initially, individuals should acknowledge and recognize their state of depression, acknowledging its presence as a condition requiring their attention and intervention. Evidently, acknowledging the need for change and accepting the existence of a problem are essential initial measures towards the path of recovery. Congratulations on recognizing the positive qualities within yourself. However, it is important to acknowledge that you are currently dealing with a psychosocial or medical condition that necessitates addressing in order to improve your well-being. This may encompass seeking professional counseling, engaging in physical activity, or undertaking any proactive measures to enhance your mental wellbeing. Prior to proceeding, it is imperative that you acknowledge the existence of the issue.

Subsequently, once you have duly acknowledged it, you can commence discerning the methods by which you intend to address said circumstances. There will, indeed, be a distinct approach to addressing each individual's circumstances, based on their preferences and aversions. An individual afflicted with depression must undertake the task of altering their mindset to overcome stagnation and pessimistic thought patterns. When it comes to individuals dealing with depression, fostering hope becomes a significant aspect in the process of reprogramming the mind. If an individual is able to discover even a small glimmer of hope amidst their circumstances, they may find that the passage of time becomes more manageable and that their perspective on the future becomes more optimistic.

Depression impacts a significant number of individuals. Nevertheless, there are individuals who encounter challenges with enduring emotional conditions that exhibit similarities to depression, albeit distinct in terms of categorization. One instance pertains to sorrow. Grief entails intricacies of trauma that primarily center around individuals, necessitating the need for those undergoing grief to find outlets for its expression. An individual experiences a profound sense of sorrow and emotional distress upon the loss of something or someone that they are utterly dependent on for their proper functioning. Numerous individuals are impacted to such an extent that they experience profound sorrow. Significant occurrences such as a particular presidential election or a catastrophic phenomenon can evoke feelings of sorrow. Grief necessitates a cognitive reorientation to acknowledge and embrace the trajectory of the grieving process. Typically, in the experience of grief, there exists a progression of stages.

Chapter 2: Fear

Within the realms of this chapter, we shall engage in a discourse concerning the phenomenon of fear, elucidating its numerous encumbrances upon one's faculties and endeavors. Each and every one of us encounters fear, as it is an inherent aspect of our being. Its purpose is to inform us of potential dangers, and its origins can be traced back to ancient times when our instinctual responses served as a means of alerting us to potential harm or unfavorable situations. In previous eras, survival hinged upon our ability to interpret fear as a vital signal indicating the immediacy of life-threatening circumstances. It is probable that you are familiar with the concept commonly known as "fight or flight." This precisely pertains to the aforementioned term. When an individual's physiological response detects a perilous or hazardous situation, it will evoke a sensation of fear. Subsequently, your physiological system will be compelled to determine whether it should engage in combat or engage in evasive action, subsequently opting for one of these courses of action.

Presently, the situation deviates somewhat from what has been previously mentioned. The majority of occasions in which we experience fear presently do not pose a threat of fatality. The apprehension that we experience subsequently impedes our progress in terms of engaging in novel experiences or unfamiliar circumstances. In the instances mentioned, although they are improbable to present any harm to us, in the event that we experience feelings of fear, we might opt to engage in a hasty retreat.

The Efficacy of Fear in Impeding Personal Progress

Fear has the potential to hinder progress and restrict personal growth if allowed to dominate one's existence. In the forthcoming section, we will explore the negative implications of fear on personal development and the pursuit of a satisfactory and meaningful life, notwithstanding its intrinsic function as a mechanism for self-preservation.

Comfort Zone

In the following section, we will examine the concept of the comfort zone. Your comfort zone pertains to the range of places, activities, objects, individuals, and various other aspects that foster a strong sense of comfort. Certain individuals opt to remain within the confines of their comfort zone, rejecting opportunities that lie beyond it, while others embrace venturing beyond this boundary, deliberately subjecting themselves to discomfort and uncertainty. For instance, in the event that an individual whom you have recently encountered extends an invitation for you to accompany them to a bar, along with their unfamiliar acquaintances, situated in a locality that is entirely unfamiliar to you. In this particular context, this event would undeniably exceed the boundaries of everyone's personal comfort level. At present, you would be confronted with a decision: whether to affirmatively respond and attend this social event despite its novelty, encompassing both unfamiliar individuals and surroundings, and to make the effort regardless. An alternative approach would entail politely declining the offer and instead seeking the company of individuals from your local community, or alternatively returning home to unwind in the comfort of your own bedroom. Although neither of these options can be deemed inherently negative, it is noteworthy that one alternative is motivated by apprehension or a reluctance to venture beyond familiar territory, whereas the other is spurred by a genuine sense of inquisitiveness and an inclination to explore uncharted territories.

While there are situations that call for it, giving in to the fight or flight response that your body has even in situations that pose no danger, can lead you to a life of saying no to every new experience or challenge and can leave you stuck in your comfort zone forever. In the given scenario, should the individual opt to reject the invitation owing to an overwhelming number of unfamiliar elements, they would essentially succumb to their body's innate fight or flight instinct and consequently choose to flee. Conversely, in the event that they are consciously aware of the fear that arises from the prospect of trying these novel activities, they may elect to proceed regardless, recognizing that such a choice is unlikely to endanger their life.

Consequently, the presence of fear serves as an impediment if one were to decline this invitation due to the accompanying opportunities forgone. Perhaps you would have encountered an individual at this establishment with whom you could have forged a profound bond, yet you have relinquished this opportunity by declining. Perhaps you might have had the opportunity to experience the musical prowess of a band that resonated with your tastes, had you attended this establishment and thus uncovered their talent. Perhaps you would have ventured into this novel community and developed a profound affection for it, subsequently making the decision to relocate there upon the expiration of your lease agreement. As you abstained from attending, it remains uncertain whether you would have developed an affinity for this locality or not. A wide array of possibilities, including but not limited to those previously mentioned, are inherent in every given scenario. Furthermore, this particular opportunity encompasses numerous novel elements, thereby amplifying the scope of potential outcomes. By confining oneself within the boundaries of one's own neighborhood, and associating solely with familiar acquaintances, the opportunities for making novel discoveries are significantly reduced. By confining yourself to your comfort zone, you are impeding your potential for numerous enriching opportunities that could significantly enhance your life. This holds true irrespective of whether you are presently experiencing fulfillment in your life or not.

Objective Establishment And The Endeavor Towards Accomplishing Those Objectives.

Goal setting and goal pursuit is another aspect that we must proceed with great caution when evaluating in our lives, ensuring that we do not view it from the same perspective as the external world. The primary concern of the observing global community is increasingly directed towards a specific desired result. Our primary emphasis should be placed not solely on the outcome, but on the comprehensive process.

Language plays a significant role in our existence - it enables communication, evokes emotions, shapes our experiences, serves as a source of inspiration, occasionally causes pain, and unveils moments of happiness. Moreover, they contribute significantly to enhancing the enjoyment and excitement of life.

It is essential for each person to understand that the attainment of any degree of achievement in life is only feasible when goals are appropriately established and plans are explicitly delineated. This is because possessing a clearly defined goal and devising a comprehensive plan in pursuit of said objective is imperative in obtaining a discerning perspective.

Once you have conscientiously undertaken the task of carrying these two elements, you will attain a lucid comprehension, which shall function as your compass given your explicit and comprehensive insight on the objectives you truly intend to accomplish.

Establishing objectives and crafting a strategic outline would provide a distinct mental representation and concurrently enable you to embed that visionary plan in your subconscious cognition. By doing so, you are simultaneously providing your subconscious mind with the appropriate guidance regarding the direction you should pursue when it pertains to carrying out your plan.

This would also provide you with the appropriate mindset for responding appropriately in the event of any unforeseen circumstances that may arise during the process; implementing this practice will help you maintain your focus undeterred even in the face of unexpected occurrences.

Maintaining concentration and adhering to your predetermined objectives is a crucial factor to bear in mind if one desires to prosper in any endeavor within their lifetime. Concentration serves as a pivotal aspect in the process of goal setting and strategic planning. This is attributable to the fact that deviating from your primary objective increases the likelihood of losing sight of all elements within your plan, ultimately culminating in the collapse of the entire endeavor.

This phenomenon occurs due to the potential confusion experienced by your subconscious mind, which leads it to infer a lack of interest in the original goal that had been ingrained within it. You would concurrently develop a dispassionate and indifferent attitude towards the objective that you were previously exceedingly enthusiastic about.

It is not effortlessly achievable nor straightforward to maintain unwavering concentration on a specific matter. In truth, maintaining unwavering concentration on a singular issue appears to be an exceedingly intricate undertaking. Why? This phenomenon arises due to the distinct identity observed within your cognition, resembling a completely disengaged and disjointed element from your central framework.

Consider it as a persistent individual who refuses to agree with your desired course of action and instead pursues its own objectives, contrary to your preferences. This is where the process of goal setting and planning can become intricate.

The crucial aspect of achieving success in the process of goal setting and planning lies in implementing measures that effectively capture and sustain one's cognitive focus and adapt to evolving circumstances. This can be achieved by maintaining unwavering commitment and steadfastness towards your objectives.

You must ensure that unforeseen circumstances should not lead you to deviate from the initial objective, but rather impact it in a way that welcomes and adapts to change, allowing you to leverage it to your advantage rather than as obstacles.

When you consistently and steadfastly engage in this practice, your mind will develop the ability to adapt to alterations and approach them with an optimistic outlook. This would lead you towards pursuing your objectives. This is the reason why maintaining a strong focus on your established goals is widely regarded as the pivotal factor that will drive you towards achieving success.

The absence of a life purpose is tantamount to lacking a sense of direction when navigating the path of life. For certain individuals, it may appear to be full of adventure. However, in the most unfavorable situation, we could potentially arrive at a point of no return where there are no feasible options to reverse the circumstances, and one must come to terms with whatever they receive for the remainder of their life.

A significant number of individuals do not desire to encounter such a circumstance in their lives. Regrettably, a considerable number of individuals perceive no viable solution to escape their current circumstances, resulting in prolonged suffering throughout their lifetimes. However, it is not widely known that individuals have the potential to transcend their adversity and experience a life of prosperity and joy.

Consider envisioning a scenario where you are devising arrangements for a vacation to a sun-kissed coastal destination; you shall embark upon meticulously organizing every element that contributes to the trip's ambiance, ensuring not just an enjoyable, but also an indelible experience.

Your entire family or companions who will be accompanying you would be enthused about the forthcoming excursion and eagerly anticipate the enjoyment at the shoreline. You may also observe that time passes swiftly, with hours appearing as mere minutes and minutes resembling mere seconds.

On the contrary, consider a scenario where you and your companions embark on a spontaneous journey, devoid of any predetermined destination. Similar to a nightmarish scenario unfolding, you might find yourself in a state of being directionless and immobilized in a space devoid of potential action. Your acquaintances express disappointment in your decision to participate in this unpleasant excursion. You experience a sense of powerlessness and embarrassment.

Each individual must engage in thoughtful deliberation and establish clear objectives in their lives regarding their intended accomplishments in both the immediate and distant future.

Envision the desired future state that you anticipate attaining in a span of five years from the present moment, and proceed to deconstruct your overarching five-year plan into manageable increments of short-term plans spanning one year each. Implementing concise plans facilitates the ability to closely monitor progress and make timely and suitable corrective actions throughout the course of the endeavor.

Self-Esteem Strategy 1 – Acquiring Insight Into The Origins Of Your Emotional State

To embark upon the journey of self-improvement and foster a sense of self-assurance, it is imperative to undertake a thorough investigation into the underlying causes that may contribute to one's dearth of confidence or presence of pessimistic notions about oneself. Carefully observe, as it is highly likely that the solutions lie within the following:

Parental disapproval

Deterioration of interpersonal connections" "Disintegration of intimate bonds" "Breakdown of relational dynamics" "Collapse of interpersonal relationships" "Degeneration of emotional connections

Being held accountable for matters.

Assuming personal responsibility for occurrences

Criticism usually originates at a certain point and often coincides with the process of maturation and personal development. Has it been conveyed to you by your parents that you have failed to meet their expectations? Did you feel unattractive in comparison to other children? Have you experienced being subject to teasing by others? Have you experienced disappointment from an individual who was expected to have affection towards you?

It is imperative for you to reflect upon your past experiences and discern the origins of the negativity that permeates your life, as only by recognizing its source can you embark upon the necessary steps to surmount it. In the event that your parents, for instance, cast a negative light upon your identity, it is imperative to comprehend that their perspective was the basis for such sentiment. Every individual holds their own opinions, yet when they project these onto others, they inadvertently expose their own deficiency instead of providing a true reflection of one's character. When faced with difficulties, parents often tend to resort to assigning blame if they are unable to effectively address the issue at hand. "I have not raised you in such a manner," or "Considering all the efforts I have invested in your upbringing." The truth is that parents occasionally induce feelings of guilt within their children due to their lack of parental experience, leading them to mistakenly attribute blame to the child instead of reflecting on their own parenting abilities. You should document the sources of negativity and express them in written form.

Exercise in understanding

It is evident that the individuals in close proximity to oneself have a significant impact on the development of our self-esteem. Please record the individuals who have influenced you and document their remarks. One must come to realize the inherent absurdity of the situation. As an illustration, in the event that a companion were to express that you exhibit a state of emotional turmoil and did so unkindly, it would not be conducive to fostering a positive sense of self-worth. Write down the name of the person who hurt you or criticized you and then write down what the criticism was. Henceforth, we shall progress and it is worth noting that, upon perusal of this written document, it shall mark the final occasion upon which you shall subject yourself to the presence of these malevolent entities. It is commendable to successfully identify the source of negativity in order to proactively steer clear of it in subsequent endeavors.

Look at your list. Comprehend it and subsequently shred it into diminutive fragments. The individuals in your vicinity who inflicted feelings of negativity upon you do not possess the authority or entitlement to do so. As you meticulously shred the words, contemplate how those negative emotions dissipate, for they persist solely as such as long as you grant them permission to do so. Today marks the auspicious commencement you have fervently sought, and you shall bravely confront the world with contentment in your authentic self. Today, we shall engage in cultivating a constructive mindset regarding your personal qualities. Through the progression of this book, we will nurture and enhance these thoughts, nurturing a sense of self-worth and fostering a genuine appreciation of your identity.

Determine which individuals within your social circle exhibit toxic tendencies. These individuals exploit or manipulate you, causing detriment to your life while offering minimal reciprocation. They are the individuals with whom you are reluctant to engage, as you are aware that they have a tendency to exploit you, while also acknowledging their lack of reciprocity. You do not exhibit a proclivity for seeking approval from others. Cease reclining and assuming the role of someone's subordinate. Determine the individuals who genuinely qualify as your close companions and allocate more of your time towards their company, while reducing your interactions with individuals who have a tendency to exploit your kindness. Learn to say "No" and don't feel guilty about it.

In the subsequent chapter, we explore the manner in which life operates from the perspective of equity. From this, you will gain insight on how to equalize the probabilities. Inequities are an inherent aspect of life, and in the event of a dearth of self-worth or assurance, it is imperative to acquire the knowledge and tools necessary to transform one's perception and outlook on life.

What Does Not Ascertain Or Define One's Intrinsic Value Or Personal Worth

When you undergo a physical examination at a medical facility, does the healthcare professional employ an arbitrary measuring instrument to determine your stature? Ideally not. Should they have made such adjustments, it is likely that your height measurement would vary between a length equivalent to 5½ sticks in one medical facility and a length equivalent to 10 sticks in a different establishment.

That sounds absurd, correct? Nevertheless, when it comes to assessing one's self-worth, many individuals rely on a comparable arbitrary benchmark.

You might not even deliberately contemplate the type of measure you utilize to assess your self-esteem. Nevertheless, it is highly probable that you are aware deep inside.

In due time, once you perceive your inherent value, self-love emerges. However, in the event that you perceive a failure to meet your intended objective, it is highly probable that your self-confidence will diminish. Hence, although you may be cognizant of these differences via your emotions, you may fail to contemplate the specific factors that exert such a profound influence upon you.

While there exist various methodologies to assess one's worth in life, it is pivotal to contemplate upon the potential drawbacks associated with certain approaches. While some individuals gauge their self-esteem based on their weight, others determine their value based on the level of attention their appearance receives. The media conveys a message akin to "your worth is determined by your appearance." Additionally, numerous promotional systems place emphasis on individuals' shortcomings, ranging from weight gain to advanced age.

Making this statement does not negate the fact that having good physical appearance can be advantageous in life. They obviously can. Nonetheless, a physically appealing physique or a captivating countenance will not endure indefinitely. The presence of hair loss, facial lines associated with aging, and weight gain in middle age can have detrimental consequences for individuals who place considerable value on their physical attractiveness.

You are probably familiar with individuals for whom their self-worth is determined by their salary or material possessions. Nonetheless, those individuals who gauge their self-esteem based on their accumulated wealth perpetually experience a sense of inadequacy.

Moreover, it is not solely individuals of wealth who define themselves by the magnitude of their financial reserves. Many individuals strive to uphold an impractical lifestyle in an attempt to attain a sense of adequacy. However, resorting to incurring debt in order to create an illusion of wealth ultimately leads to negative consequences.

Although merchandise and ventures possess financial value, they do not inherently reflect the inherent worth of an individual. There exist several distinct methodologies through which individuals depend on others to provide them with excellence. While one person may find satisfaction in being in a romantic relationship with oneself, another might seek validation from others by associating with notable figures in order to boost their self-esteem.

Some individuals may experience a sense of gratification when they surround themselves with distinguished individuals. A comprehensive roster of personal connections and a busy calendar of social engagements contribute to their sense of self-worth and importance.

Dependent upon others for one's sense of fulfillment is akin to pursuing an elusive objective. You have no jurisdiction over the perceptions others hold of you, and it is simply impossible to consistently fulfill everyone's expectations. You will consistently find it difficult to receive sufficient recognition and positive feedback to truly cultivate self-approval.

Engaging in a profession allows a multitude of individuals to experience a sense of productivity. To be frank, the majority of individuals introduce themselves by stating their profession, for instance, by saying, "I work as a software engineer for PC systems," or "I am employed as a legal advisor." Their occupation does not merely define their job; rather, it serves as a fundamental aspect of their identity. Their occupation suggests that they hold a position of importance.

Based on the level of your self-confidence, discussing your professional designation poses a major risk. A temporary decline, sudden shift in employment opportunities, or significant health problem could hinder your career trajectory and contribute to a profound identity crisis. Certainly, if your sense of self-worth is closely tied to your professional status, even a meticulously planned retirement could potentially have a devastating impact. If one's self-esteem has been consistently dependent on one's occupation, the absence of that vocation will likely result in a negative self-perception.

In certain instances, it is imperative for individuals to be recognized solely for their achievements. The individual who proudly showcases her latest business accomplishment may derive a sense of satisfaction when she elaborates on her achievements. However, an individual who is unable to cease commiserating over a mistake they have committed may encounter difficulty in making progress, as they have not achieved the intended outcome that would have provided emotional relief. Although it is customary to experience a sense of delight in one's accomplishments, basing your entire self-worth on the outcome is akin to constructing a residence upon an unstable groundwork. You must attain consistent achievements in order to foster self-approval, which entails avoiding actions that may lead to failure.

The manner in which you gauge your self-worth determines the type of lifestyle you will lead. Employ a measure that relies on variables within your jurisdiction rather than external factors beyond your influence in the realm of existence.

When one attains a firm understanding of their personal identity and experiences contentment with their evolving individuality, they shall traverse life's inevitable highs and lows with an overarching sense of harmony. Regardless of being terminated, going through a divorce, or failing to secure a promotion, you will still possess self-assurance.

Instead of seeking temporary sources of confidence, evaluate your self-esteem based on your highest level of self-identity. Continue in accordance with your principles and forge a purposeful and significant existence.

The subsequent, amidst a multitude of other factors, do not inherently determine your intrinsic value.

The Distinction Between Self-Esteem And Confidence

You will encounter several disparate definitions in various sources. Self-esteem, self-assurance, self-approval, self-value, self-perception, and self-identity are only a handful of examples.

Many individuals may express that they experience a deficiency in confidence or possess diminished self-esteem. Presently, a multitude of responses can be found upon entering the query into a search engine such as Google or by perusing scholarly articles on the respective topics, which I have already undertaken. I have consequently generated a synopsis based on acquired knowledge, and more significantly, from firsthand experience.

Confidence
When individuals express a dearth of confidence or assert that another individual lacks confidence, I inquire,

"Pray tell, confidence in what endeavor or aspect?"

Confidence may pertain to a particular facet of one's life or to one's overall approach to life. One might possess confidence in their abilities as an author, yet lack assurance in their singing prowess—such is the case with myself. In other words, a person may feel self-assured in a particular talent while lacking such conviction in another.

One illustration is my capacity to effectively engage and communicate with individuals from diverse backgrounds, which has significantly improved over time due to deliberate efforts on my part.

In addition, one may possess confidence in a certain area while harboring low self-esteem or general confidence in regard to the majority of other aspects in their life.

For example, there have been instances in my previous employment where my responsibilities entailed delivering progress reports during meetings. Through these experiences, I honed my abilities in public speaking, thus enhancing my efficacy in delivering charismatic presentations.

It signified my assurance in presenting my discourse, attributed to incessant refinement of my charisma methodologies, yet intermittently I grappled with markedly diminished self-assurance. I have been exposed to instances where authoritative supervisors exhibit a lack of appropriate treatment towards their subordinates, and despite their outwardly displayed confidence in their professional capacities, they possess a diminished sense of self-worth, resulting in the projection of these insecurities onto others.

To acquire a substantial level of confidence, one must engage in deliberate and consistent practice, tirelessly honing their skills and adaptability to achieve personal growth. The most expedient means of enhancing one's skills is to procure the guidance of a mentor who possesses profound knowledge and can impart their wisdom and experience.

One's overall conviction in their approach to life largely depends on their overall perception of their capabilities in life. This is derived from the extent to which you hold yourself in high regard and possess a positive self-perception, leading to the development of self-esteem. Confidence does come from results and results come from taking action (even if you don't feel like it). Nevertheless, a heightened sense of assurance stems from harboring a positive self-perception irrespective of the eventualities or achievements, thereby leading us to the subject of self-esteem... which holds significant significance especially when our endeavors fail to yield the desired outcomes.

Self Esteem

If one cultivates a strong sense of self esteem, there is a higher probability of approaching matters with assuredness. Initially, one may encounter some difficulty when attempting new skills; however, it is essential to make an attempt and acknowledge that one can solely strive to improve. Should I choose to partake in ballroom dancing, I am aware that my initial efforts may present some difficulties, and I understand and accept this fact. It is not indicative of my incompetence as an individual; rather, it signifies my lack of expertise in that particular domain. In contrast, my closest companion, however, ventured into the realm of ballroom dancing on a whim, and has demonstrated considerable skill in the endeavor. This attribute is among the factors that contribute to his status as my closest companion, as he demonstrates a remarkable willingness to explore uncharted territories and possesses a consistently optimistic outlook on life.

Self-esteem pertains to an individual's personal assessment, encompassing their level of self-approval or self-liking, and incorporates their self-acceptance, self-worth, and self-concept.

Self-acceptance or self-worth pertains to one's ability to embrace oneself in the present moment.

I have encountered hardships in this aspect, as I have consistently possessed a strong drive for success, and when I am unable to attain monumental objectives, I do not experience fulfillment.

The concept of self pertains primarily to the extent of one's worth to society and the perceived capacity to contribute. In my personal experience, this has generally proven to be satisfactory as I have established personal objectives and displayed a strong drive for success.

Insufficient self-acceptance or worth can have a pervasive impact on one's overall self-esteem.

In summary:

Self-esteem refers to the assessment one makes of oneself, involving aspects such as self-worth, self-acceptance, and self-perception in the present moment. Self-acceptance, self-worth, and self-concept are synonymous with self-esteem.

Self-acceptance and self-worth pertain to one's current perception and appraisal of oneself.

In the realm of self-perception, one's self-concept encompasses both their perception of their image and the intrinsic worth they perceive themselves to possess in relation to the world.

Confidence can be defined as an individual's perception of their proficiency in a particular skill or aspect of life. However, it is probable that individuals with greater self-esteem will possess elevated levels of general confidence when facing various endeavors.

Mindset

Given that this represents the book's title, it is certainly important for me to elucidate the concept of mindset as presented in this literary work. One's mindset encompasses their perception of life and self. Consequently, this culminates in the choices and subsequent actions one takes in their personal journey. The intention of this book is to assist you in cultivating a mindset that is imbued with robust self-esteem and unwavering confidence.

Chapter 1: Self-Esteem
What is self-esteem?
Self-esteem refers to an individual's personal and introspective appraisal of their intrinsic value and emotional state. It pertains to the perception one holds of their own self and the evaluative standpoint one adopts towards oneself. The amalgamation of one's self-perception and personal convictions gives rise to their self-esteem.
Certain sentiments individuals may experience in relation to themselves encompass feelings of pride or shame, triumph or defeat, and exhilaration or despair. Certain beliefs that individuals hold about themselves may encompass notions such as "I possess inherent goodness," "I lack competence," or "I deserve worthiness." Self-esteem fundamentally represents one's own perception and evaluation of oneself.
How is it developed?

The general consensus among experts is that the accumulation of experiences spanning one's entire lifespan, starting from childhood and extending into adulthood, serves as the foundation for either positive or negative self-esteem. The development of a child's self-esteem is greatly influenced by the actions and guidance of their parents. If a child is bestowed with unwavering love, their sense of self-worth will be robust and they will experience a profound feeling of being esteemed and nurtured. Juvenile individuals engage in the practice of evaluating themselves against their peers, not only in terms of scholastic performance, but also with regards to attirement, conduct, and interpersonal engagements.

As children develop, those who benefit from the presence of supportive and nurturing adults who have effectively established firm boundaries and expectations exhibit the highest levels of self-esteem. During adolescence, the establishment of friendships and the development of relationships gain significant importance as they contribute significantly to the formation of self-esteem in young individuals. Confidence serves as an effective indicator of one's self-esteem. If your child exhibits a sense of assurance and possesses strong, meaningful bonds with others, it is probable that she possesses a solid level of self-worth.

What factors impede the cultivation of self-esteem?

Numerous occurrences arise throughout one's life that can impede the cultivation of self-esteem, with a significant portion manifesting during childhood. I have briefly explored a few of these topics earlier, and we will delve into them further in subsequent chapters. Extensive research has been conducted on the subject of self-esteem development and the factors that detrimentally affect its progression.

Research findings indicate that the development of self-esteem in both men and women manifests similarly, exhibiting equivalent rates without any discernible disparities. Insufficient cognitive development, health-related issues experienced during childhood, or a disadvantaged socioeconomic background can adversely influence the development of self-esteem throughout an individual's life. The development of a healthy self-esteem is detrimentally affected by stress, depression, and Post Traumatic Stress Disorder (PTSD).

Dealing with Shame

Shame is among the primary contributing factors to individuals experiencing diminished self-esteem. Feelings of shame often manifest during early childhood and have the potential to persist throughout an individual's lifetime. Furthermore, these feelings can be instigated by seemingly spontaneous actions or events. Children who have experienced abuse often develop a sense of shame, while those who exhibit any form of difference, such as height, weight, skin color, or introversion, may also experience feelings of shame.

When an individual, be it a child or an adult, perceives a lack of appreciation or acknowledgement within their respective group or groups, it often leads to the experience of shame. This phenomenon results in a reduction in self-confidence. In the event that your child experiences exclusion from their peers during their time in junior and senior high school, it is probable that they will endure feelings of isolation and potentially become a target of bullying. As a consequence, a significant decline in self-esteem and the emergence of self-doubt ensue.

Harassment and Ramifications of Diminished Self-Confidence

As evidenced by increasing occurrences in our society, the act of bullying can have severe and profound effects on an individual's self-worth, sometimes culminating in tragic outcomes such as suicide. Even after the individual ceases to endure the torment, the repercussions on their self-worth persist over a prolonged period. Occasionally, there are stark repercussions on one's self-esteem, whereas in other instances, the consequences may be concealed or suppressed.

Certain repercussions of bullying encompass a diminished sense of confidence or a pervasive self-doubt. The person feels "not good enough" in one way or another. Self-reflection is additionally a consequential outcome of bullying as a consequence of internalizing the bully's derogatory remarks. This holds particularly true in cases where the bullying pertains to the physical attributes of the individual subjected to it.

A number of adverse consequences can arise from the act of bullying, such as:
• Nocturnal enuresis
• Social isolation • Seclusion • Solitude • Detachment
• self-inflicted death • intentional taking of one's own life • voluntary act of ending one's own existence

Summary and Action Plan

Self-respect constitutes a crucial aspect of our inherent constitution as individuals, albeit one that can be challenging to comprehensively grasp. It pertains to the introspective and affective assessment of an individual's personal value. Self-esteem is comprised of the sentiments we experience towards ourselves and the convictions we hold regarding our own worth.

Action Plan

• Gain an understanding of Abraham Maslow's Hierarchy of Human Needs, and discern the placement of self-esteem within this hierarchical structure; appreciate the significant role self-esteem plays in the lives of individuals. https://en.wikipedia.org/wiki/Maslow%27s_hierarchy_of_needs

• Employ the utilization of a journal as a means to document instances of shame, while striving to discern the root causes that induce such emotions.

- Locate an individual within your personal circle with whom you can openly express your emotions and who genuinely offers assistance with identifying factors that provoke distress.

Positive Thinking

What Is Positive Thinking?

Presently, it is imperative to acknowledge that the concept of positive thinking does not entail surrendering unquestioningly or feigning ignorance about adverse circumstances. This does not imply that you must devise a method by which you persistently elude the truth or persistently evade confronting these internal issues. This does not imply that one must exist with utmost naivety, refusing to acknowledge the possibility of any mishaps or suppressing one's dislike towards any undesired occurrences.

The practice of adopting a positive mindset enables one to acknowledge the occasional unpleasantness of life. It affords you the opportunity to recognize occasions where things may be amiss or require modification. Nevertheless, the underlying premise is that positive thinking addresses these circumstances in a constructive manner rather than resorting to avoidance. Rather than attempting to evade or exacerbate a problem, you will cease your efforts and endeavor to identify the most productive approaches through which you can effectively engage with the world around you.

Typically, the cultivation of positive thinking commences with one's internal dialogue. It pertains to the persistent internal dialogue persistently occurring within, dictating one's thoughts, thought processes, and reasons to uphold the existing patterns of thinking. It centers on the notion that one will engage in self-dialogue that mirrors their prevailing mindset. Individuals who exhibit positivity tend to possess a constructive attitude and optimistic thought patterns, whereas those with a negative disposition often engage in self-deprecating internal dialogues. They will harbor the notion that they lack proficiency in any endeavor or that they possess inadequate potential for achievement, and ultimately, they tend to internalize these beliefs.

Self-dialogue and soliloquies predominantly stem from personal experience. The manner in which one has encountered the world shapes their perception of the external environment, resulting in hindrances when attempting to effectively engage with others. This poses a significant issue if you already exhibit a proclivity towards pessimism. Upon examining the manner in which you engage with yourself, it is often possible, through the process of introspection, to establish a clear connection to past experiences. It is possible that your parents may have never shown their approval towards you, or you may have experienced a lack of genuine friendships where others truly appreciated you. Perhaps you harbored alternative motivations for experiencing such sentiments. Nevertheless, the introspective dialogue one cultivates will undoubtedly influence their interactions with the surrounding environment.

When one adopts such a pessimistic mindset, they tend to become ensnared in a cycle from which escape is seemingly impossible. Your pessimism will inevitably attract further negativity in due course. Nevertheless, the contrary holds true too—when one adopts a positive mindset, it becomes a catalyst for attracting additional positivity into their life, thereby instilling confidence in their ability to sustain such constructive thoughts. You shall not experience a sense of entrapment or imprudence; instead, you will discern opportunities for perpetual progression.

Chapter 7

Practice Self-Management

After self-awareness, comes self-management.

Self-management entails the capacity to exert conscious control over one's actions, guiding oneself towards a specific objective with careful consideration and mindfulness.

Let us endeavor to reflect upon a moment in time when you exercised a measured and advantageous judgment despite the transient frenzy instigated by our emotions. Can you honestly remember? How frequently did you subsequently engage in this behavior once you became cognizant of it?

As demonstrated earlier, it is notable that the neurochemical process occurring within the brain during moments of heightened emotional intensity typically transpires rapidly, preceding the activation of the cognitive faculties responsible for rational deliberation. This is the very reason why encounters with individuals experiencing intense emotions often lead to instances of irrationality and occasionally foolish errors. Consequently, young couples who are consumed by intense emotions often choose to elope or hastily enter into matrimony. Our propensity to act irrationally has led us to engage in conflicts that could have been preventable had we dedicated sufficient time to contemplation before taking action. This reason could potentially be the cause behind individuals experiencing employment termination and fractured personal relationships.

However, once the practice of self-awareness is initiated, complying with this second aspect becomes considerably more manageable. If any such connection exists, it is unequivocally linked to one's level of self-awareness. Once you develop an understanding of the factors that incite a reaction within you, you will enhance your ability to evaluate circumstances and implement proactive strategies for managing your behavior when faced with provocation from others or challenging events.

By electing to be emotionally engaged, you will acquire the capacity to receive distressing information or endure challenging circumstances without jeopardizing your ability to think logically.

Therefore, for individuals experiencing challenges with managing anger, enhancing self-awareness would involve recognizing the factors that incite rage within oneself. Then, self-management follows through. Given that you possess the cognizance of the factors that incite your anger, you will commence making informed choices aimed at preemptively addressing your anger prior to its consummate dominance over you.

In the event that you experience a high level of apprehension, you will acquire an understanding of the underlying causes of your anxiety and subsequently adopt a more intentional approach to conquering it.

However, to proceed with this phase, you will require dedication and a significant amount of deliberate contemplation. Due to our inherent preference for stability, the human mind often dissuades us from embracing any form of transformative action. Indeed, it is your own psyche that impedes your progress towards attaining higher accomplishments.

Change is scary. As a consequence, you will discover a preference for remaining within familiar territory. The prospect of adopting a conscious approach to one's movements and interactions in the world can be an intimidating undertaking. This will result in your subsequent discomfort with the activities that previously brought you pleasure. It entails acknowledging one's shortcomings and developing a heightened understanding of the impact of one's unconscious behaviors on both personal relationships and overall psychological well-being. Hence, undertaking the endeavor of regulating one's emotional responses is anticipated to be challenging. Moreover, there is an inherent sense of immense gratification that derives from expressing one's emotions. You believe that your actions are warranted. The surge of adrenaline experienced during that moment imbues a heroic quality to one's actions. You exhibit admirable audacity and bravery, rather than succumbing to mere sentimentality and irrationality. Therefore, it is possible for individuals to develop an addictive inclination towards perpetuating this pattern of emotional unrest. However temporary it may be, the long-lasting repercussions of an emotional response to any given circumstance are apparent.

Upon attaining a heightened awareness of your emotions, you will develop the capacity to extend forgiveness to individuals who are grappling with their own challenges, fostering a genuine desire to provide assistance to them. As one cultivates self-forgiveness, does their capacity for forgiveness toward others also increase? When one lacks emotional harmony, it becomes evident in their interactions with others. You find yourself experiencing anger towards another individual due to your own propensity for having a short fuse. You deride another individual who harbors fear due to your own affliction with trepidation. These various challenges contribute to rendering you incapable of being treated and socially withdrawn.

Enhancing one's emotional management skills leads to a heightened ability to engage with others effectively. Instead of reducing individuals to their emotional state, you perceive their hardship by recognizing that it is a challenge you have also encountered or currently face, and therefore, can empathize. Subsequently, you effortlessly radiate charm by virtue of comprehending the emotional state of the other individual and aiding them in embarking upon their initial endeavors to enhance their emotional regulation.

Chapter 4

The Evolution of Your Self-esteem and Confidence

The development of self-confidence can be attributed to either inherent qualities or external influences commonly referred to as "nature or nurture." In this context, "nature" pertains to the environmental conditions in which an individual was raised, whereas "nurture" denotes the quality of care and upbringing one received. Confidence is cultivated through a series of experiential milestones that enable individuals to excel or attain proficiency. Accordingly, a man has the capacity to cultivate self-assurance in various domains. Nevertheless, the advancement may be impeded by the individual's self-perception. Therefore, it is of utmost importance to prioritize the cultivation of self-esteem in the realm of personality development.

The Impact of Nature and Nurture on Self-esteem

Home and relationship

One's initial conception of self is fostered within the confines of their own residence. The manner in which both parents interact with their child is contingent upon the nature of their interrelationship. A child who is afforded the courtesy of being listened to and spoken to with respect acquires the ability to reciprocate the same level of courtesy at an early stage of development. He experiences a sense of appreciation, leading to the cultivation of a robust self-esteem. Similarly, a child who is subjected to severe criticism or neglect experiences the development of an inferiority complex, as they are persuaded that their actions and abilities are consistently inadequate.

Authority Figure

Parents, guardians, educators, mentors, and any influential figure in a child's life play a pivotal role in shaping a person's self-perception. Commendation, endorsement, acknowledgement, recompense, and a constructive stance towards errors committed establish the groundwork for cultivating a robust sense of self-worth.

Likewise, a child can experience emotions of failure and insufficiency when exposed excessively to demands for flawlessness. Low academic scores, unsuccessful performance in a game, or even minor errors made by an individual are perceived as indications of personal failure.

Experience of abuse

Few things have a stronger impact on one's self-esteem than the ordeal of abuse, whether it manifests through physical, emotional, verbal, or sexual means. In the absence of a robust network of support, he will eventually develop hostile tendencies toward himself. Bullying exemplifies the perpetration of abusive behavior. The manner in which parents or guardians respond to a child's encounter with bullies significantly impacts their child's sense of self-esteem. A child who endures mistreatment within their own household from their parents or siblings may perceive bullying in any other environment, such as school, as an expansion of their negative domestic encounters. This experience merely reinforces his conviction that he lacks competence and has no value.

In contrast, readily disregarding a child's distressing encounter creates difficulties for the child in establishing trust in others. On the opposing side, one finds a propensity towards excessive vigilance. This fails to instill in a child the necessary moral compass to effectively safeguard themselves independently. Conversely, he will persist in seeking an authoritative figure to offer assistance.

Belief System

This phenomenon is commonly associated with religious convictions, particularly those that place excessive emphasis on feelings of inadequacy, sins, guilt, and other negative self-perceptions. This phenomenon is also observed among collectives where individuals are made to feel inadequate in the absence of organizational backing. Continued exposure to this type of association has the tendency to alter an individual's perception of their own identity. It fosters an adverse reliance on the belief system and a lack of confidence in one's own capabilities.

Media and Society

In contemporary society, particularly due to the pervasive influence exerted by the media, there exists a prevailing dominance in shaping individuals' perception of what is deemed "good, beautiful, and acceptable." The definition of beauty has come to be narrowed down to the possession of a flawless physique, while the attainment of success is often equated with material accumulation and worldly wealth. As children's exposure to the media's skewed representation of values increases, they experience heightened feelings of inadequacy when unable to meet societal expectations.

Chapter Seven: Enhance your self-esteem to elevate your self-confidence

Fortunately, there exists a superior alternative. An alternative course of action would be to focus on improving your self-esteem. Put simply, it is imperative that you focus on elevating your self-assurance by initiating a comprehensive internal transformation. Through establishing a firm bedrock of self-esteem and self-regard within oneself, one is subsequently able to emanate these qualities outwardly, culminating in an elevated state of assurance and poise. Will this occur expeditiously? No. Is this easy? The level of comfort may vary among individuals, yet it remains a task that necessitates exertion. It, nonetheless, requires a certain degree of consistency and constant struggle.

How Does This Work?

To cultivate self-confidence by enhancing self-esteem, it is essential to initiate a shift in one's self-perception. You alter your self-perception and the perspective through which you perceive yourself. Everybody has self-perception. Each individual carries a mental representation of their own identity, their abilities, and their future trajectory. Furthermore, we possess an illustration representing our position within the broader context. Put simply, we possess a strong comprehension of our own sense of place. Individuals who experience a deficient sense of self-assurance evidently possess unfavorable perceptions concerning these matters. They perceive their position as being situated at the lowest point. They perceive themselves as having little to no value. They hold the belief that any attempt they make will yield mediocrity. In essence, they maintain a humble perspective and do not consider themselves to possess any extraordinary qualities.

It is crucial for you to engage in the improvement of your self-perception. You must alter your self-perception. You need to transition from perceiving yourself as a constant recipient of external circumstances beyond your influence to becoming an individual who proactively orchestrates outcomes. This represents a significant advancement in one's personal understanding and evaluation. One transitions from a state of passive observation as life unfolds, to envisioning oneself as an active participant who holds a direct influence over the course of events. Once more, you transition from being an observer filled with frustration towards the outcomes of your life, to constantly questioning the transformation of the proactive individual within you.

This can be attributed to individuals' self-perception. What is your self-perception? What is your self-perception? What type of self-image do you possess in your mind? This sense of self-awareness plays a critical role in shaping one's self-identity. When you establish your self-concept, you ascertain the boundaries within which you operate. You have the power to ascertain your own capabilities. You embody either the factors that impede your progress or those that propel it. The most favorable aspect of this situation is the inherent sense of agency vested in you, as it is you who determines the parameters, as opposed to an external party.

Altering Your Story

Another essential component in the process of enhancing self-confidence, related to cultivating self-esteem, pertains to the necessity of altering one's personal account or narrative. As previously indicated within the contents of this literary work, it is expounded that the narrative of your personal depiction remains an enduring tale that traverses your consciousness. This is the foundational principle or narrative structure that you adhere to. Your narrative serves as a lens through which all of your experiences and interactions with the external world and its inhabitants are interpreted and shaped.

For instance, if you hold the belief that you are unwelcome upon entering a room, and if individuals cast upon you a specific facial expression, it is probable that you would perceive it as a cynical gaze. The manner in which others observe you implies that it would be advisable for you to refrain from involvement. You are not welcome in this place. Go away!

Should your viewpoint be that you possess inherent worth and your presence brings forth positivity, it is likely that you perceive that same glance as an opportunity to present yourself. Perhaps you could perceive it as an opportunity to create a positive impact. Irrespective of the circumstances, one invariably finds oneself in a completely distinct location. Rather than experiencing feelings of insignificance, unworthiness, exclusion, rejection, and dissatisfaction, you may perceive it as an impartial opportunity for engagement. One could perceive it as a favorable occasion, perhaps even an advantageous prospect. Do you comprehend the significance of your narrative?

Your narrative holds significant importance in shaping your perception of reality, as it is worth noting that what we commonly perceive as objective truths are, in fact, subjective judgments. That is the extent of their capabilities. Two individuals have the ability to perceive a given set of information and form two completely distinct understandings. The variance in these interpretations is contingent upon the narratives they employ. In the process of cultivating self-confidence by enhancing self-esteem, it becomes imperative to replace one's personal narrative. In order for this internal transformation to be effective, it is imperative that precise alterations are made in your personal narrative.

Self-regard refers to an individual's perception and evaluation of oneself. If one is repeatedly informed throughout their life of their clumsiness and internalizes this perception, it will inevitably shape their self-perception as a clumsy individual. The reality is that much of the feedback we receive throughout our lives is not malicious in nature, but rather has the potential to leave a lasting impact on us for many years. To illustrate, my mother consistently refrained from recognizing any of my accomplishments as meritorious. During my formative years, I held the belief that I was devoid of certain qualities or attributes that my peers possessed, as my efforts consistently went unrecognized. The presence of acknowledgement is not necessary for our confidence, but it does serve to enhance it. When continually disregarded for our positive actions, we have a tendency to incline towards a pessimistic stance. We harbor a sense of dissatisfaction regarding our personal identities, and when confronted with novel obstacles, we frequently falter due to our inherent self-doubt.

This phenomenon may begin as soon as an individual reaches toddlerhood, and it is important to note that parents do not intentionally engage in such behavior, despite its occurrence. An analogous phenomenon ensues within educational settings. You are subject to comparative evaluation with your peers, leading you to question your ability to meet your own personal standards. You do not possess the same level of aesthetic beauty as other individuals. You do not possess natural athletic abilities. You lack the capability to perform tasks that others are able to accomplish. The issue lies in the fact that there will inevitably exist individuals who outperform you in certain aspects of their lives. It is inevitable, thus how do you address this matter. Ultimately, the extent to which that unfavorable perception of you is reinforced will determine the outcome.

Consequently, when information is consistently relayed to individuals, they are inclined to regard it as factual, subsequently adopting corresponding thought patterns. Have you ever encountered individuals who have become ensnared in a harmful and exploitative relationship? When individuals experience a deficiency in their confidence and self-esteem, they tend to perceive themselves as deserving less than their counterparts, thus accepting subpar circumstances. Individuals with a vulnerability in their character tend to attract individuals who engage in abusive behavior. Even if one manages to exit such a relationship, if their self-assurance remains low, there is a high probability that subsequent relationships will yield similar negative consequences. This recurrence stems from the individual's internalized expectation and the ongoing manifestation of their self-perception throughout their life. If one believes that their value is limited to the challenges life presents them, they might content themselves with collecting mere crumbs, overlooking their potential entitlement. I have some information to share with you. While this might have been the customary practice for you, it is not regarded as obligatory. One has the ability to alter their own perception of oneself, thereby enhancing self-esteem and confidence simultaneously.

Firstly, let us examine the adverse consequences associated with self-esteem issues:

• You do not place sufficient importance on your own worth.
✓ You abstain from indulging in items or experiences that you perceive as undeserved.
• You hold the belief that you are entitled to a lesser position or treatment in life compared to others.
• You are content with subpar relationships • You accept unsatisfactory relationships • You lower your standards for relationships

- You compromise on positions that do not allow you to showcase your talents and abilities

At a certain juncture in one's existence, it becomes imperative to emancipate oneself from the shackles of negativity. Upon successfully doing so, the ability to cultivate an unwavering sense of self-assurance emerges, as confidence operates in such a manner. When you successfully perform a task with excellence, it instills a sense of self-satisfaction. If you reside within an environment where you consistently undertake mundane responsibilities due to harboring a lack of confidence in your ability to achieve greater endeavors, your experiences will be confined solely to such mediocre tasks. To some degree, the internal imagery of your self greatly influences the type of existence you lead.

Hence, it can be inferred that self-esteem serves as the determinant of one's life quality. When the level is diminished, there are minimal expectations and limited outcomes. If one possesses a significant level of self-regard, they demonstrate an unwavering determination to pursue their goals and ambitions with utmost assurance and resolve. There is an additional tine present in the utensil as well. Individuals who exhibit excessive self-assurance tend to perform tasks hastily and are prone to errors, primarily due to their inflated perception of their own abilities. Moreover, such individuals typically remain unaffected by feedback, as their self-esteem remains relatively impervious to criticism. Criticism per se does not inflict harm. It contributes to personal growth, facilitates the establishment of personal limits, and promotes learning. However, solely resorting to self-judgment can have a detrimental impact on one's self-esteem and confidence.

In the upcoming chapters, we will thoroughly investigate the cause and effect of various occurrences, while offering strategies to foster personal growth. By enhancing your comprehension of the detrimental effects of low self-esteem and lack of confidence, you will be equipped to make positive changes in your life. The manner in which you perceive your own life is equally responsible as the manner in which individuals criticize and belittle you. Once one achieves mastery over oneself, external validation becomes unnecessary, thereby allowing self-esteem to flourish and prosper. Rest assured, you possess the capability to tackle this matter, however, acquiring the necessary knowledge is imperative.

Chapter 10: A Strategic Blueprint for Introvert Achievement

An introverted individual is more likely to overcome their fears and flourish in social settings if they possess a well-defined plan to direct their actions. Additionally, it is recommended to create a strategic framework that can be utilized to commence the cultivation of your social identity.

Set a goal

Your initial objective entails establishing a goal for your social engagements. Your goals should be related to the social activities that you have been neglecting in the past. As an illustration, should you have experienced a prolonged period without engaging in social outings, it would be advisable to establish the objective of actively participating in dating activities until you successfully achieve the desired outcomes pertaining to your romantic pursuits. If your business network is limited, it is imperative to actively seek out opportunities to forge connections with individuals within your respective industry. You should meet someone new every week. The objective you establish is contingent upon the aspects of your social life that you have previously overlooked.

Embrace and cultivate your introverted attributes.

If you continue to harbor negative perceptions regarding your introversion, it would be advantageous to revise them.

It is advisable for you to begin deriving pleasure from solitude without harboring any feelings of guilt. In a social situation, it is advised to maintain a composed demeanor and contribute to the conversation at your own pace, ensuring your comfort level. However, it is important not to excessively censor your thoughts.

Rather than consistently projecting an extraverted persona, it would be advisable to exercise moderation in employing extraverted traits, reserving them primarily for significant endeavors that contribute to your objectives.

www.ingramcontent.com/pod-product-compliance
Lightning Source LLC
Chambersburg PA
CBHW050251120526
44590CB00016B/2309